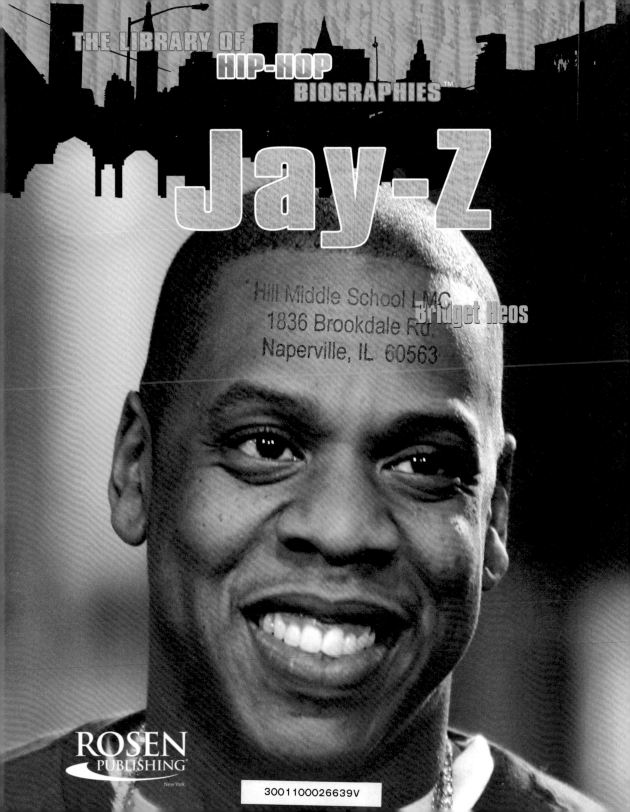

THE LIBRARY OF **HIP-HOP BIOGRAPHIES**™

Jay-Z

Bridget Heos

ROSEN PUBLISHING®
New York

To my sons, Johnny, Richie, and J. J., and my husband, Justin

Published in 2009 by The Rosen Publishing Group, Inc.
29 East 21st Street, New York, NY 10010

Library of Congress Cataloging-in-Publication Data

Heos, Bridget.
Jay-Z / Bridget Heos.—1st ed.
    p. cm.—(The library of hip-hop biographies)
Includes bibliographical references and index.
ISBN-13: 978-1-4358-5052-1 (library binding)
ISBN-13: 978-1-4358-5438-3 (pbk)
ISBN-13: 978-1-4358-5444-4 (6 pack)
1. Jay-Z, 1969– —Juvenile literature. 2. Rap musicians—United States–Biography—Juvenile literature. I. Title.
ML3930.J38H46 2009
782.421649092—dc22

[B]

2008010577

Manufactured in the United States of America

On the cover: Born Shawn Carter, hip-hop artist and producer Jay-Z has sold over thirty-three million albums since 1996.

CONTENTS

INTRODUCTION

Jay-Z has rapped in the past that he's not a businessman—he's a business, man.

That is true. He has cranked out a chart-topping album nearly every year since 1996. He is part owner of the New Jersey Nets and cofounder of Roc-A-Fella Records. Until recently, he was president and chief executive officer (CEO) of Def Jam Recordings. He is a multimillionaire. It seems everything Jay-Z touches turns to gold. Now, people seek him out for projects, most recently, to create a companion CD for the movie *American Gangster*.

And, to think, it all started with a green notebook.

As a kid, Jay-Z wrote rhymes constantly. Only back then, he was known as Shawn Carter. He lived in the Marcy Houses projects of Brooklyn, New York, with his mother and three siblings. He described the neighborhood as having the worst schools, the worst roads—the worst of everything. It was difficult not to lose hope.

It was the 1980s. Crack had taken hold in the neighborhood. Most people Shawn knew were either using drugs or selling them. He never used crack, but he became a drug dealer. At the time, he wanted to better his situation. Only later did he think about the destruction it caused his neighborhood.

A turning point in Shawn's life was when his father left the family. Besides the financial hardship this caused, Shawn, just eleven years old, didn't open up to people after that. He had idolized his dad. Shawn didn't want to be hurt again.

But he had another way to express himself: rap. His talent eventually provided an escape from the dangerous world of drug dealing.

To this day, Jay-Z is known not for his voice, which even he says is not that great, but for his lyrics and flow. He took West Coast gangsta rap and made it grittier. He rapped about being the kid on the corner who risked dying and hoped for a better life.

CHAPTER ONE

IT'S A HARD KNOCK LIFE

When Shawn Carter was a kid, his mother's friend gave him a green notebook. It was unlined, so the words he wrote were crooked. He had tiny hand-writing, so nobody could read what he wrote.

But even then, he wrote constantly. Sadly, Shawn lost the notebook. But he remembered one rhyme, which he revealed in *Rolling Stone* magazine in the November 2007 issue: "I'm the king of hip-hop/Renewed like the Reebok/The key in the lock/With words so provocative/As long as I live."

He laughs about those lyrics now. But perhaps the years of writing as a child were the practice Jay-Z needed to be the artist he is today.

Born in 1969, he grew up listening to Al Green, Prince, Stevie Wonder, and early rappers like Jimmy Spicer. His mom and dad had huge record collections. When they had parties, Shawn and his siblings would peek into the room and watch the grownups enjoying the music.

Shawn, the youngest of four siblings, was a happy-go-lucky kid.

Growing up, Jay-Z listened to soul singer Al Green, seen here performing in the mid-1970s, as well as rock, R & B, and rap greats.

He was a good student. He played basketball and dice with his friends. His mom pushed him to do his best in school. His dad showed him the way home from different places. Shawn's nickname was Jazzy because he was a jazzy little dude.

But the neighborhood he grew up in—Marcy Houses in the Bedford-Stuyvesant area of Brooklyn—was tough. In fact, it was one of the most dangerous places in America. At age nine, Shawn witnessed a murder. But that wasn't the first time he heard gunshots. Drugs and violence had taken hold of the neighborhood. Still, his parents kept a close watch on him.

WHERE HAVE YOU BEEN?

Then, everything got harder. Shawn was eleven years old when his father left the family. It changed him. In his lyrics, he said that his teachers couldn't reach him and his mom's discipline couldn't match the pain his dad caused by leaving.

His song "Where Have You Been?" is about a son confronting his father. In it, the son talks about how the family couldn't eat right after the dad left—food stamps didn't buy enough good food.

Music was a way for Shawn to say what was on his mind. He drummed out rhymes on the kitchen table late at night. He couldn't rest until he wrote down what he needed to say. He also studied the dictionary, searching for words that rhymed.

Shawn's mom encouraged him by giving him a boom box. In his song "December 4" (his birthday), his mother narrates parts of his life. One thing she says is that the boom box was her way of keeping him close to her and out of trouble. The loudness of it drove his older siblings crazy, though.

Jay-Z attended George Westinghouse High School with the Notorious B.I.G., shown performing here in 1995. The two rappers became close friends and collaborated on songs until B.I.G.'s tragic murder in 1997.

The practice paid off. In the neighborhood, Shawn was developing a reputation. Even then, his friends knew that his style was unique. He rapped fast, and his lyrics were full of ideas and pictures.

The part of Brooklyn where Jay-Z is from had its share of rappers. He attended what some people call "Hip-Hop High School." Its real name is George Westinghouse High School. The Notorious B.I.G., Busta Rhymes, and Jay-Z all went to school there. But talent was not necessarily a ticket out of the neighborhood.

NICKNAMES

- Jazzy: Jay-Z was called this as a kid because he was a jazzy little dude. He changed it slightly to be what it is now.
- J-Hova/Hov: This is a play on the name Jehovah. It's Jay-Z's way of saying he's the god MC.
- Jigga/Jiggaman: So that a song could be played on the radio, Jay-Z changed a derogatory word for African Americans to say, "Jigga what? Jigga who?" Some people thought that was still offensive. Jigga is also a nickname Jay-Z gave himself.
- S Dot: Jay-Z sometimes refers to himself as this in songs. It's the first initial of his name, as in S. Carter.

CAN I LIVE?

Seeing no other way out of the ghetto, Shawn sold drugs, starting at about age sixteen. He has talked about this decision in his lyrics. In "Pray" on the companion CD for the movie *American Gangster*, the teenage narrator describes seeing drug needles on the ground on his way to his homeroom. His dad leaves the house to find the man who killed his uncle. A drug dealer rolls up in a fancy car. The police stop the dealer, only to ask for a bribe. Then, the narrator asks people to pray for him and for God to forgive him because he's choosing that life. Or, as Jay-Z rapped on "December 4," the life chose him.

Some critics say that Jay-Z and other rappers don't just write about dealing drugs. They boast about it. And they don't talk enough about the bad things that happen because of their crimes.

But in songs like "You Must Love Me" and "D'Evils," Jay-Z is not bragging. He is talking about heartbreaking regrets and bitter realities. He told *Rolling Stone* in October 2007 that he tries to tell both sides of being a hustler.

"There's pitfalls: you might go to jail, you might get shot," he said. "And you're messing with the community. You gotta deal with that."

Now that he is older, Jay-Z told *Rolling Stone*, he understands the pain and mental struggle that addicted people go through. At the time he was selling drugs, he just thought the customers were dumb.

Like a lot of songwriters, themes from Jay-Z's life repeat in many of his records. He also rapped about the dangerous life of drug dealing in "Can I Live" on his first album, *Reasonable Doubt*.

But rewind. *Reasonable Doubt* would not come about until he was twenty-six years old. Getting to that point was an uphill battle. Sometimes, the young Shawn Carter would make the climb only to get kicked to the bottom.

RAP GAME/CRACK GAME

Shawn still wrote constantly. Standing on the corner, he jotted down rhymes on scraps of paper he had in his pocket. When the paper ran out, he memorized the rhymes until he could go somewhere to write them down. Eventually, he was able to memorize entire songs. The last song he wrote down was "Can I Live." Today, he composes lyrics in his head and records them for the first time in the sound booth.

But he has told his nephew, an aspiring rapper, to write every single day. A basketball player practices every day. A writer should, too.

Shawn's first job as a rapper was being the sidekick for another rapper in the neighborhood: Jaz. It was 1989, and Shawn was known as the champion rapper of the neighborhood. He joined Jaz for what seemed like a promising career. Shawn was featured in the music video "Hawaiian Sophie" and traveled to London with Jaz. But things didn't pan out.

Jaz, a tough-looking guy from the Marcy projects, was being marketed like the next "Fresh Prince of Bel-Air." It was not a good fit. The record didn't sell well, and the label dropped Jaz.

Shawn also toured with Big Daddy Kane, hoping it would lead to a record deal. It didn't. Feeling dejected, he moved home and returned to selling drugs. Rap wasn't working out. He started asking himself whether his failure was telling him something: he wasn't good enough. But he had good friends. And they told him a different message: don't give up.

Rapper and record producer Big Daddy Kane helped jump-start Jay-Z's career.

CHAPTER TWO

CAN'T KNOCK THE HUSTLE

The aspiring rapper who came to be known as Jay-Z was shot at three times in one day. Incredibly, none of the bullets hit him. They might have even saved his life. Because that's when Jay-Z turned to a less dangerous hustle: rap.

He has said that as a street dealer, you're playing Russian roulette with your life. But financially, trying rap again was a risk. At that time, rappers didn't make a lot of money. He defended his decision to try rap in the song "Can't Knock the Hustle," the hustle being rap. In it, he said people shouldn't criticize the way a person puts food on the table.

It was the early 1990s when Jay-Z started recording with hip-hop icon DJ Clark Kent. Through him, he met Damon Dash, an entrepreneur from Harlem.

By this time, rap already had "old school" songs like "Rapper's Delight" and "You Be Illin'." Rap was introduced in the 1970s, when DJs rapped over songs and scratched beats on turntables as party music.

Hip-hop legend DJ Clark Kent helped Jay-Z start his career by working with him in the recording studio. He also introduced him to Harlem entrepreneur Damon Dash, who became Jay-Z's manager.

Soon, artists were rapping about street realities. In the early 1980s, Grandmaster Flash and the Furious Five's "The Message" described a child growing up in the ghetto, wanting to have money like the drug dealers, and finally, dying young.

In the same decade, Boogie Down Productions paved the way for both gangsta rap and, after a member of the group was murdered, socially conscious rap. This kind of rap talks about racism and other social problems. It offers sometimes radical solutions. When the group Public Enemy came on the scene, it seemed like socially conscious rap would be the wave of the future.

But in 1989, N.W.A. took rap in the other direction.

GANGSTA GANGSTA

N.W.A.—a group that included Ice Cube, Eazy-E and Dr. Dre— rapped about, and often glorified, the gangster lifestyle on the album "Straight Outta Compton." Like Public Enemy, they commented on social problems, such as police roughing up black teens. At this time, the Los Angeles Police Department was cracking down on gangs, and black kids as young as twelve were often stopped by police. Some of the boys felt like no matter what they did, the police assumed they were in a gang. The music was a way to fight back.

But unlike socially conscious rappers, N.W.A. also talked about violence like it was a game. In "Gangsta Gangsta," they rap about going to a party and pulling a gun on anyone who looks at them wrong.

Eventually, the group split up. Ice Cube and Eazy-E went solo. Dr. Dre formed Death Row Records with Suge Knight. Gangsta rap, named for the N.W.A. song "Gangsta Gangsta," on the other hand, was here to stay.

Even rappers who didn't live the gangster life still sang about it. In fact, Ice Cube, who wrote many N.W.A. lyrics, didn't grow up hustling. His mom and dad worked at the University of

California, Los Angeles. He attended college for a short time to study architecture. Still, he represented a new voice in music. He was the most controversial and acclaimed gangsta rapper of his time.

Dr. Dre is considered one of the pioneers of gangsta rap with fellow N.W.A. members Ice Cube, Eazy-E, DJ Yella, and MC Ren.

In the 1990s, gangsta rap changed. N.W.A. often made gangsta-hood sound like a party—a nightmarish one, but still a party. New artists like Tupac Shakur, known as 2Pac, and the Notorious B.I.G., on the other hand, described drug dealing as a business they chose reluctantly. It was their only ticket out of poverty. In a way, they were living the life described in "The Message."

Some people called this "crack rap." Violence and sexism were still glorified, but now there was an acknowledgement of the consequences. Friends might die. Innocent kids might die. And the hustler's own life was at risk, too. And, as in the songs of N.W.A., there was still talk about the reasons why people turn to crime: they grow up in neighborhoods that get the worst of everything. And they want a better life.

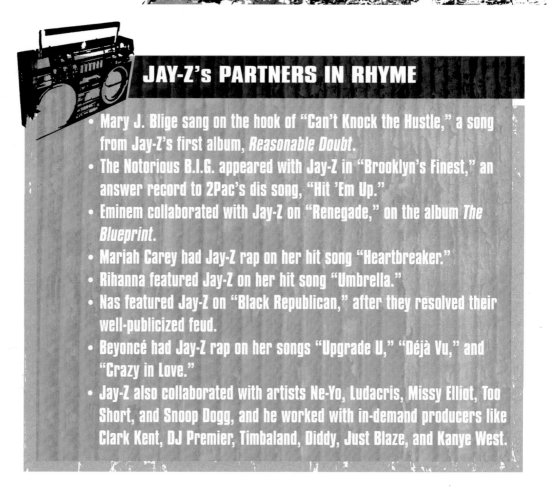

JAY-Z's PARTNERS IN RHYME

- Mary J. Blige sang on the hook of "Can't Knock the Hustle," a song from Jay-Z's first album, *Reasonable Doubt*.
- The Notorious B.I.G. appeared with Jay-Z in "Brooklyn's Finest," an answer record to 2Pac's dis song, "Hit 'Em Up."
- Eminem collaborated with Jay-Z on "Renegade," on the album *The Blueprint*.
- Mariah Carey had Jay-Z rap on her hit song "Heartbreaker."
- Rihanna featured Jay-Z on her hit song "Umbrella."
- Nas featured Jay-Z on "Black Republican," after they resolved their well-publicized feud.
- Beyoncé had Jay-Z rap on her songs "Upgrade U," "Déjà Vu," and "Crazy in Love."
- Jay-Z also collaborated with artists Ne-Yo, Ludacris, Missy Elliot, Too Short, and Snoop Dogg, and he worked with in-demand producers like Clark Kent, DJ Premier, Timbaland, Diddy, Just Blaze, and Kanye West.

ROC BOYS

Jay-Z was perhaps the best lyricist of the crack rap era. Some say he is the best MC ever. But that didn't mean getting signed on a record label was easy.

For one thing, the West Coast—with Dr. Dre's G-funk sound and breakout stars like Snoop Dogg—dominated rap, which originated on the East Coast. Also, Jay-Z's fast rhymes were different from what people were used to hearing. They didn't know what to make of them.

With Damon Dash as his manager, Jay-Z toured New York, where he grew in popularity. Singles such as "In My Lifetime" were an underground success. His unique style was becoming an asset. But finding a wider audience took time.

Jay-Z's first song to play on the radio was "Dead Presidents." Next, "Ain't No," featuring Foxy Brown, got national attention when it was chosen for *The Nutty Professor* movie soundtrack. The song was produced by Jay-Z's old friend Jaz. Now known as Jaz-O, he never made it as big as his one-time sidekick, but he is still active in the music business.

Meanwhile, Jay-Z, his friend Kareem "Biggs" Burke, and Damon Dash decided to make things happen on their own terms. Jay-Z never got a record deal. So, the three friends started the company Roc-A-Fella Records to produce Jay-Z's music themselves.

Jay-Z released his first album, *Reasonable Doubt*, in 1996. It didn't top the charts, but it is considered a hip-hop classic. It also featured Biggie Smalls, later known as the Notorious B.I.G. Having grown up in the same neighborhood, Jay-Z and Biggie became fast friends. When Rock-A-Fella signed a partnership deal with Def Jam Recordings, Jay-Z had arrived.

West Coast rapper 2Pac (Tupac Shakur, *left*) and Suge Knight of Death Row Records were shot in their car after a Mike Tyson fight in Las Vegas. Knight survived, but Shakur did not. Six months later, the Notorious B.I.G. was also shot and killed.

TWO DEATHS

But in the rap world, a rivalry between East Coast and West Coast record companies turned serious. At first, Suge Knight of Death Row Records and Sean "Puffy" Combs of Bad Boy Records exchanged insults, but the artists they represented—2Pac and the Notorious B.I.G.—were friends. That is, until 2Pac was robbed and shot while visiting a studio where the Notorious B.I.G. and Puffy were also working. 2Pac was convinced that B.I.G. and Puffy set him up.

In the song "Hit 'Em Up," 2Pac made vicious threats. Together, the Notorious B.I.G. and Jay-Z responded with the record "Brooklyn's Finest."

"Dis" records are common in rap. But what happened next shocked hip-hop musicians and fans. After a September 1996 Mike Tyson fight in Las Vegas, 2Pac was murdered in a drive-by shooting. Six months later, the Notorious B.I.G. was killed after a party in Los Angeles. He, too, was shot in a car when a man drove up alongside him.

Some believe that a rivalry between the record companies, the rappers, or gangs led to the murders. There were several theories. In the end, neither murder has been solved.

Not only had Jay-Z lost a friend in the Notorious B.I.G., but hip-hop was also mourning the violent deaths of two of its biggest stars. Many considered 2Pac to be a poet and prophet. And with wit and charisma, the Notorious B.I.G. was well-loved, too.

When he died, the Notorious B.I.G. was not only a talented rapper but also a pop star. His album "Ready To Die" sold more than four million copies. It brought East Coast hip-hop back into the limelight, after West Coast rap had topped the charts for so long. Sadly, it also foretold a tragically young death.

Rap fans wondered who would be the next voice for the kid on the street.

CHAPTER THREE

A GHETTO ANTHEM WITH A BROADWAY BEAT

Working with Sean "Puffy" Combs, Jay-Z gave his next album, *In My Lifetime, Vol. 1*, more of a pop flavor. The album still had hard-core raps, but some people thought records like "Sunshine" were too fluffy. The album sold better than *Reasonable Doubt*, but some fans thought Jay-Z was selling out.

Musically, he was at a crossroads. Did he stay true to his smart, hard-hitting lyrics? Or, did he soften his sound to sell more records? Could he find a way to do both? The video for "Streets Is Watching" showed that Jay-Z still had street cred. It reassured his original audience that he was a rapper, not a pop star.

Jay-Z went on tour with Combs, then known as Puff Daddy, but it didn't go well. The venues were half empty. The facilities for Jay-Z and his crew fell short of expectations. Jay-Z was ready to leave the tour.

But it's a good thing he stuck around a little longer, because that's when he heard the beat for "Hard Knock Life." Kid Capri, the DJ between sets, was playing it. Jay-Z was coming off the stage, and people were hugging and congratulating him. But all he could hear was the music.

The song, written in 1977, was from the Broadway musical *Annie*. It tells the story of a red-headed orphan in Depression-era New York. She eventually gets adopted by billionaire Daddy Warbucks. Jay-Z thought lines in the song about getting tricked instead of treated were perfect for a street anthem. Also, he liked that the singing orphans were not sad. Instead, they were stating the facts—and making the best of their situation.

Jay-Z said in a song that he made more money when he dumbed down his lyrics. It's a common conflict in arts and entertainment. People like what they understand. Artists want to keep it real. But they won't make money unless people like their art. So, the artists dumb it down.

"Hard Knock Life" got lots of radio play. It was even parodied by the Mike Myers character Dr. Evil in the third *Austin Powers* movie. Whether Jay-Z dumbed down his lyrics at this point—or ever—is a matter of opinion. Grammy voters didn't think so. *Vol. 2: Hard Knock Life* was named Best Rap Album of 1998. However, Jay-Z boycotted the awards show. He said that it overlooked rap artists year after year.

At that time, many of the rap awards were not even televised. The Grammy Awards would later change its tune. By 2003, four out of five best song nominees featured rappers, including Jay-Z on Beyoncé's "Crazy in Love."

GUILTY UNTIL PROVEN GUILTY

When Jay-Z pled guilty to stabbing a record executive, he considered it a wake-up call. He didn't want to lose it all. He put his criminal days behind him.

The year after "Hard Knock Life" came out, Jay-Z and his Roc-A-Fella partners started Rocawear, a line of high-end urban clothing. Selling mostly online, the company grossed one hundred million dollars in the first eighteen months. It seemed Jay-Z had the Midas touch.

But old ways were not easily forgotten. The same year, Jay-Z was accused of a serious crime. He was charged with assault for stabbing record executive Lance Rivera in a Times Square night-club. Apparently, Jay-Z thought Rivera was bootlegging his music. Rivera recovered and was released from the hospital the next day.

At first, Jay-Z said he was innocent. He released the song "Guilty Until Proven Innocent" to show his disgust with being tried in the court of public opinion. But in the end, he pled guilty. He got three years probation. The civil suit was settled out of court.

The stabbing surprised music journalists, who thought Jay-Z's songs about violence were cautionary tales. Also, reporters always considered Jay-Z to be a laid-back, nice guy. He later said that the incident was a wake-up call. It made him realize how quickly he could lose it all. But he didn't.

JAY-Z'S MESSAGE TO KIDS

As rap artists became more successful, Jay-Z saw a problem facing young people. Kids used to have unrealistic plans to be professional athletes. Now, they wanted to be rappers instead.

Jay-Z toured the country telling urban high school students that this was an even more unrealistic goal. While there were two hundred National Basketball Association (NBA) players making a living, only ten to twenty rappers consistently made money in the business.

His message: do the math. Get your education. To help young people achieve this goal, he gives college scholarships to kids from his old neighborhood through the Shawn Carter Scholarship Fund.

H.O.V.A.

Jay-Z started to put out at least one new album every year, including *The Blueprint*, one of his most critically acclaimed works. Hit singles included "The Blueprint (Momma Loved Me)," which he has said is the song that best describes his real life.

"Izzo H.O.V.A." was another favorite record on the album. "Hova" is a play on "Jehovah"—he was calling himself the god MC. But not everybody worshipped him.

When *The Blueprint* came out, Jay-Z was one of the most dissed rappers out there. Nas, Prodigy, and Judakiss all took swipes at him. Jay-Z said that disses like these didn't mean anything. If rappers really had a problem with each other, they wouldn't put it in a song for the world to hear. He said beefs between rappers only show how competitive the game is. Jay-Z and fellow New York rapper Nas competed fiercely for years.

His next album was *The Blueprint 2: The Gift & the Curse.* Critics didn't like this album as much, and even Jay-Z later said that it had too many songs. One song on the album, "'03 Bonnie & Clyde," a 2Pac cover, featured Jay-Z's real-life girlfriend, Beyoncé Knowles.

CRAZY IN LOVE

Jay-Z and Beyoncé come from different worlds. Beyoncé is from a middle-class family in Houston, Texas. Jay-Z is from the mean streets of Brooklyn, New York. Beyoncé's father became the

Grammy winners Jay-Z and Beyoncé dated for six years before marrying in 2008. Their intimate and elegant wedding was held at Jay-Z's New York City penthouse.

manager of her R & B group, which eventually became Destiny's Child. Jay-Z used street smarts and help from his friends to make it in the rap world. But talent-wise, they have a lot in common. Both have won Grammys. And both have combined songwriting and performing skills to make it to the top of the game.

Jay-Z tries to keep their relationship private. "It's difficult enough to have a relationship with your relatives involved," he told *Rolling Stone* in the November 29, 2007, issue. "To have millions of people involved—that's messed up!"

But he told interviewer Charlie Rose about the first time he saw Beyoncé. She was rapping with Wyclef Jean. Jay-Z said the first thing he noticed about her was her talent. Her ability amazed him.

They have collaborated on several projects. Beyoncé was in Jay-Z's video for "December 4." And Jay-Z rapped on Beyoncé's song "Crazy in Love." For "Déjà Vu," Jay-Z even came out of retirement to record with Beyoncé. The couple married in 2008.

But wait a second. Jay-Z retired? When? Why?

FADE TO BLACK . . . FOR A WHILE

By the time *The Blueprint 2* came out, Jay-Z had ghostwritten songs for Dr. Dre, Puff Daddy, and Will Smith, and he sung a number-one duet, "Heartbreaker," with Mariah Carey. He was putting out a hit record every year. Creatively, what more could he do?

Also, by this time, Jay-Z had bought his mom a house and had purchased a penthouse overlooking Manhattan. He had moved his family out of the projects. But he knew he couldn't rap forever. It had been his plan all along to pursue business after rap.

He was already successful in this area. Def Jam would soon buy Roc-A-Fella Records, and Rocawear was distributing clothing as far away as Japan. Still, Jay-Z wanted to take his skills further.

He made *The Black Album*, which included the hit single "99 Problems." He performed at Madison Square Garden in New York City. There, he gave the mothers of Tupac Shakur and the Notorious B.I.G. checks for their sons' foundations. Then, in the documentary *Fade to Black*, he announced that he was retiring from recording. That movie now makes Jay-Z cringe because, well, he didn't retire. Not for long anyway.

But before Jay-Z came out of creative retirement, he took on a new challenge. He became the president and CEO of Def Jam Recordings in 2004. In that role, he helped several musicians achieve stardom, including Young Jeezy, Rihanna, and Ne-Yo.

Jay-Z told Charlie Rose that being an artist made him a better record executive. Like a coach who used to play ball, he had been on

By 2002, Rocawear, Jay-Z's line of hip-hop clothing, was being shown on New York's hottest runways and sold in countries all over the world.

the court. He knew the challenges of creating music.

In this case, the coach wasn't ready to quit playing the game. From childhood, Jay-Z couldn't stop writing rhymes. As an adult, his creative drive didn't weaken. Soon, he came out of retirement.

CHAPTER FOUR

OUT OF RETIREMENT AND INTO THE KINGDOM

Jay-Z had to settle something. He has said that beefs are OK—as long as they don't go too far. They can even inspire rappers to improve their game. But his feud with rapper Nas had dragged on forever.

So, coming out of retirement in 2005, Jay-Z staged a New York concert called "I Declare War." The stage was set up like the White House's Oval Office, and there was even a red phone to release a nuclear bomb (not really, of course). But at the end of the night, Jay-Z told his fans that the concert was about something bigger than war. It was about peace.

Jay-Z came out of retirement in 2005 for the "I Declare War" concert, where he performed with Memphis Bleek, seen here on the right, and other artists. The audience realized that the night was really about peace when Jay-Z and New York rapper Nas ended their longstanding feud with an onstage hug.

He and Nas, both New York rappers, performed together. Afterward, they hugged.

At this time, rappers from the South, such as Lil' John & the East Side Boyz and Ludacris, were rising on the charts. And rappers from the Midwest, such as Kanye West (from Chicago), Nelly (from St. Louis), and Eminem (from Detroit), were making their mark, too. Now, New York was ready to take back the rap game.

But for Jay-Z, the takeover didn't go as well as planned. He put out a new album, *Kingdom Come*, which was different from his other work. He became famous rapping about hustling. But his life had changed drastically since he made *Reasonable Doubt*. The lyrics on *Kingdom Come* reflected that. Now, Jay-Z sang about the spoils of success. The album was nominated for a Grammy, but critics didn't like it. They said that, at times, the raps sounded like a rich person bragging.

"MY ADIDAS" AND OTHER ENDORSEMENTS

One criticism of the album was that Jay-Z talked too much about name brands. Rapping about luxury goods is nothing new. In 1979, the Sugar Hill Gang rapped about Lincoln Continentals and Cadillacs.

People talk about the good old days, when rappers sang about simple pleasures like sneakers. But even then, endorsements were happening. Run-DMC got $1.5 million after making "My Adidas." And even before rap, making money by making music was the goal. After all, it's called show *business*.

Today, hip-hop artists endorse everything from Verizon Wireless phone service to Tommy Hilfiger clothing. Sometimes, the artists are paid. Other times, they name-drop for free because they like the products or hope to get an endorsement later.

Some have said that Jay-Z and other hip-hop artists take advertising—free or paid—too far in their songs. But for others, the problem with rap isn't the commercialism. It's the offensiveness.

HIP-HOP UNDER FIRE

Hip-hop was under fire in 2007. Leaders in the black community and members of Congress criticized rappers for using racially offensive words and for disrespecting women in their lyrics and videos.

It all started when white shock jock Don Imus called black members of the Rutgers University women's basketball team

Don Imus (*left*) was interviewed by Reverend Al Sharpton (*right*) after the shock jock made derogatory comments about African American members of the Rutgers University women's basketball team. That led to discussions about what should be done about rap lyrics, which are often disrespectful to women.

derogatory names. He was eventually fired. This started a debate about whether rappers should also be held accountable for disrespecting women in their music.

During a roundtable discussion on *The Oprah Winfrey Show*, *New York Daily News* columnist Stanley Crouch asked if women should have to suffer just so that rappers could get rich. *Kansas City Star* columnist Jason Whitlock said that rappers disrespected themselves in their music, too. He said that no culture in history was respected without first respecting itself.

Jay-Z wasn't on the show for this discussion, but elsewhere, he defended the gritty lyrics that hip-hop artists write. He said that rap didn't make Don Imus a racist. In fact, he probably couldn't even name Wu-Tang Clan's first album. Jay-Z said that if people wanted to talk censorship, they should do it across the board— from movies to the Internet—and not just single out hip-hop.

Jay-Z also said that people should look at who makes the songs: mostly young men coming from bad neighborhoods. They're angry. They haven't matured yet. And they're telling the truth.

But they're also exaggerating, he said. Jay-Z ends one of his songs by reminding people that rap is just entertainment. He said that songs should be looked at along the same lines as movies. Just because the actor—or singer—says things, it doesn't mean it's his personal opinion. The rapper is narrating a story.

Nowhere is that more true than on Jay-Z's 2007 album, *American Gangster*. Songs are written mostly from the viewpoint of Frank Lucas, a 1970s' gangster.

JAY-Z'S BUSINESS ENDEAVORS

- Cofounder of Roc-A-Fella Records, a multimillion-dollar company.
- Cofounder of Roc-A-Fella Films, which makes everything from short dramas such as *Streets Is Watching*, to comedies such as *Death of a Dynasty*.
- Cofounder of urban clothing line Rocawear.
- Co-owner of the distributing rights to Armadale Vodka.
- Co-owner of the New Jersey Nets.
- Owner of the 40/40 Club, a chain of elite sports bars in New York, Atlanta, Las Vegas, Tokyo, and Macau.
- Endorsement or partnership deals with companies including Reebok (the S. Carter shoe), Hewlett Packard (computers), Motorola, Verizon, GMC, and Cherry Coke.

IF JAY-Z HAD FALLEN

Jay-Z said that he loved the gray area in the movie *American Gangster*. Frank Lucas was a ruthless gangster, but he took care of his family. The "good guys" were really bad guys (corrupt police officers), and the "bad guys" were good guys. (To make things even grayer, police officers have since sued the movie company, saying the film distorts the facts.)

Jay-Z made the record not as a soundtrack, but as a companion CD. Songs delve into the emotions the character of Frank Lucas must have felt during moments in the film.

Jay-Z said the album opened emotions he hadn't felt in a long time. It also gave him a chance to imagine what might have been if he hadn't stopped dealing drugs. Eventually, he would have gone to jail or died—a fate he describes in the song "Fallen."

Critics have said that *American Gangster* is Jay-Z's best album since *Reasonable Doubt*. He took new chances with this album. He worked again with Sean Combs, now known as Diddy. But instead of having a pop flavor, the album sounds like something totally new. Jay-Z combined rap with 1970s' soul and a live horn section. The beats reflect the adrenaline-fueled life of a high-rolling gangster.

He hasn't said whether he will retire after this album. He retired as president and CEO of Def Jam Recordings but is still an artist for the label. Jay-Z has said that he still hoped to make history in the music business.

BIG BROTHER

Creatively, he has already left his mark. When *American Gangster* came out, Jay-Z tied Elvis Presley for having ten number-one albums on the Billboard 200. Only the Beatles have more (nineteen).

His protégés are faring well, too. In 2007, Def Jam Recordings artists scored twenty-six Grammy nominations, including five for Jay-Z. One nomination was for Rihanna's song "Umbrella."

Kanye West, who got signed as an artist after being a producer for Jay-Z, is one of the hottest rappers today. Besides being critically acclaimed, he is frequently in the news for saying whatever is on his mind.

He wrote a song about Jay-Z called "Big Brother." In it, he expresses mixed feelings about Jay-Z. West looked up to the rap star but felt disappointed when Jay-Z wouldn't give him tickets to his show. Also, West said that after he told Jay-Z he was collaborating with Coldplay, Jay-Z copied him.

You might think Jay-Z would hate this song. Nope. Instead, he thinks it's West's best song since "Jesus Walks." (Jay-Z defended himself on the ticket issue, though. He said that he gave West four free concert tickets. When West wanted two more, Jay-Z told him to buy them because it was a charity event.)

In a September 19, 2007, article on www.sohh.com, Jay-Z said, "I think it's a fair portrayal from a little brother's perspective."

He said Roc-A-Fella is about tough love. "It's nothing given," he said in the same article. "Everyone has to work for theirs, and that's how you make strong individuals, by not carrying them. That's how you make a Kanye West. You make him fight for his position."

The strategy seems to have worked for Jay-Z's recording artists. And it worked for Jay-Z, too. People call him the ultimate rags-to-riches story, but it's not that simple. For Jay-Z, there was no Daddy Warbucks. Of course, his friends helped him along.

Since retiring as president and CEO of Def Jam Recordings, Jay-Z has still had many business interests. He is co-owner of the New Jersey Nets and a real-estate investor, among other things. People will watch to see what the artist and entrepreneur does next.

But he had to work hard, believe in himself, and finally start a business in order to achieve success.

Today, Jay-Z is co-owner of the New Jersey Nets and a real-estate investor. He has mingled with the rich and powerful—from Bono and Bill Gates, to former U.S. president Bill Clinton and Senator Barack Obama. Showing interest in world affairs, he worked with the United Nations to make the documentary *The Diary of Jay-Z in Africa: Water for Life*. It is about the lack of clean water that many people in the world face.

Fans, businesspeople, and community leaders are watching to see what Jay-Z will do next. Whatever it is, it will likely combine his artistic vision and stone-cold business skills. With Jay-Z, you can't knock the hustle. For real.

TIMELINE

1969 Shawn Carter is born on December 4. He spends most of his childhood in the Marcy Houses projects in Brooklyn, New York.

1981 At age eleven, Shawn and his family suffer a blow when his father leaves them. Meanwhile, rap has emerged as a new music sensation. Shawn expresses his feelings through rhymes, which he is constantly writing.

1986 At about age sixteen, Shawn becomes a street hustler. While standing on the corner, he writes rhymes on scraps of paper. Nicknamed Jazzy, and then Jay-Z, he is known as the best rapper in the projects.

1988 *Yo! MTV Raps* brings hip-hop music further into the mainstream.

1989 The phrase "gangsta rap" is coined after the release of N.W.A.'s record *Straight Outta Compton*. Meanwhile, Jay-Z's friend Jaz is signed to a record label and Jay-Z becomes his sidekick. When the label drops Jaz, Jay-Z goes back to hustling. He later tours with Big Daddy Kane, but that does not lead to a record deal.

1993 Jay-Z starts selling demo tapes to mom-and-pop shops.

1996 Jay-Z, Damon Dash, and Kareem "Biggs" Burke start Roc-A-Fella Records. They find a distributing company. Jay-Z releases *Reasonable Doubt*. "Ain't No" becomes a hit single and is featured in the movie *The Nutty Professor*.

1997 Jay-Z's second album, *In My Lifetime, Vol. 1*, sells more copies than his first.

1998 *Vol. 2: Hard Knock Life* features a remix of a Broadway song from the musical *Annie*. It is a crossover hit.

1999 Jay-Z and his partners found Rocawear, a line of luxury street clothes. Jay-Z is accused of stabbing record executive Lance Rivera. The man recovers from the injury. Jay-Z later pleads guilty.

2001 Jay-Z releases one of his most critically acclaimed albums, *The Blueprint*.

2003 After putting out an album every year, Jay-Z retires from making music. He goes on a farewell tour and makes the documentary *Fade to Black*.

2004 Jay-Z becomes president at Def Jam Recordings. Roc-A-Fella is bought out by the parent company, Universal.

2005 Jay-Z comes out of retirement with the concert "I Declare War." He makes peace instead with rival rapper Nas.

2006 Jay-Z releases *Kingdom Come*, which critics dislike.

2007 Jay-Z releases *American Gangster*, a companion CD to the movie of the same name. Some critics say the album tells a better story than the movie. At the end of the year, Jay-Z retires as president of Def Jam Recordings.

SELECTED DISCOGRAPHY

1996	*Reasonable Doubt* (Roc-A-Fella Records)
1997	*In My Lifetime, Vol. 1* (Roc-A-Fella Records)
1998	*Vol. 2: Hard Knock Life* (Roc-A-Fella Records)
1999	*Vol. 3: Life and Times of S. Carter* (Roc-A-Fella Records)
2000	*The Dynasty: Roc La Familia* (Roc-A-Fella Records)
2001	*The Blueprint* (Roc-A-Fella Records)
2001	*MTV Unplugged* (Roc-A-Fella Records)
2002	*The Best of Both Worlds* with R. Kelly (Roc-A-Fella Records)
2002	*The Blueprint 2: The Gift & the Curse* (Roc-A-Fella Records)
2003	*The Blueprint 2.1* (Roc-A-Fella Records)
2003	*The Black Album* (Roc-A-Fella Records)
2004	*Collision Course* with Linkin Park (Warner Brothers)
2006	*Kingdom Come* (Roc-A-Fella Records)
2007	*American Gangster* (Roc-A-Fella Records)

GLOSSARY

CEO The chief executive officer, or top leader, of a company.

crack rap A grittier form of gangsta rap, in which lyrics delve into the realities of drug dealing.

DJ Short for "disc jockey," who, in rap, creates the beats.

endorsement A business deal in which a famous person earns money by promoting a product.

gangsta rap A style named after the N.W.A. record *Gangsta Gangsta*, in which lyrics talk about the gangster lifestyle.

hip-hop A movement that encompasses many arts, from graffiti to break dancing.

MC Short for "master of ceremonies," recalling the days when rap was something DJs did over turntables at a party.

producer In rap, the creator of beats for records. Some producers, such as Timbaland and Kanye West, also become rappers.

product placement A form of advertising in which someone is paid to feature an item in a song, video, movie, or TV show.

rap Part of the hip-hop movement in which artists rhyme over beats, often about thought-provoking, controversial, gritty, or funny topics.

R & B Short for "rhythm and blues," a style of music that was influenced by the blues and is the basis of rock and roll.

street cred A person's reputation among peers.

FOR MORE INFORMATION

Roc-A-Fella Records
Web site: http://www.rocafella.com
Founded by Jay-Z, Damon Dash, and Kareem "Biggs" Burke.

The Shawn Carter Scholarship Fund
P.O. Box 1898
Radio City Station
New York, NY 10101-1898
Web site: http://scartersf.org
Jay-Z gives college scholarships to kids from the Brooklyn
    neighborhood where he grew up.

Web Sites

Due to the changing nature of Internet links, Rosen Publishing
has developed an online list of Web sites related to the subject
of this book. This site is updated regularly. Please use this link to
access the list:

http://www.rosenlinks.com/lhhb/jayz

FOR FURTHER READING

Abrams, Dennis. *Jay-Z* (Hip-Hop Stars). New York, NY: Checkmark Books, 2007.

Bankston, John. *Jay-Z* (Blue Banner Biographies). Hockessin, DE: Mitchell Lane Publishers, 2004.

Barnes, Geoffrey. *Jay-Z* (Hip-Hop). Broomall, PA: Mason Crest Publishers, 2007.

Chang, Jeff. *Can't Stop Won't Stop: A History of the Hip-Hop Generation.* New York, NY: St. Martin's Press, 2005.

Chuck D., Yusuf Jah, and Spike Lee. *Fight the Power: Rap, Race, and Reality.* New York, NY: Dell Publishing, 1997.

Haskins, James. *One Nation Under a Groove: Rap Music and Its Roots.* New York, NY: Jump at the Sun, 2000.

Light, Alan, ed. *The Vibe History of Hip-Hop.* New York, NY: Three Rivers Press, 1999.

Lommel, Cookie. *The History of Rap Music* (African-American Achievers). New York, NY: Chelsea House Publications, 2003.

Paniccioli, Ernie, and Kevin Powell. *Who Shot 'Ya? Three Decades of Hip-Hop Photography.* New York, NY: HarperCollins, 2002.

Zephania, Benjamin. *Gangsta Rap, A Novel.* New York, NY: Bloomsbury, 2004.

BIBLIOGRAPHY

Bahrampour, Tara. "New York: Manhattan: Rapper Pleads Guilty." *New York Times*, October 18, 2001. Retrieved January 15, 2008 (http://www.nytimes.com).

Barboza, Craigh. "Friend or Foe?" *USA Weekend Magazine*, January 28, 2001. Retrieved November 27, 2007 (http://www.usaweekend.com/01_issues/010128/010128jayz.html).

Bruno, Anthony. "Hip-Hop Homicide." TruTV Crime Library. Retrieved January 25, 2008 (http://www.crimelibrary.com/notorious_murders/celebrity/shakur_BIG/index.html).

CBS News. "The King of Rap." August 13, 2003. Retrieved January 25, 2008 (http://www.cbsnews.com/stories/2002/11/18/60II/main529811.shtml).

Chang, Jeff. *Can't Stop Won't Stop: A History of the Hip-Hop Generation*. New York, NY: Picador, 2005.

Cromelin, Richard. "Jay-Z—Back to Brooklyn." *Minneapolis-St. Paul Star Tribune*, November 16, 2007. Retrieved November 28, 2007 (http://www.startribune.com/music/story/1553911.html).

Forero, Juan. "Police Arrest Hip-Hop Star in a Stabbing at a Nightclub." *New York Times*, December 3, 1999. Retrieved January 15, 2008. (http://www.nytimes.com).

Norris, Chris. "Damn, It Feels Good to Be a Gangster." *Blender*, December 2007. Retrieved December 18, 2007 (http://www.blender.com/guide/articles.aspx?ID=2962).

Rodriguez, Jayson. "Jay-Z, Behind the Rhymes: Hov Reveals Why He Hasn't Written Down Lyrics in a Decade." MTV. Retrieved November 26, 2007 (http://www.mtv.com/news/articles/1574995/20071126/jay_z.jhtml).

Rolling Stone. "Jay-Z Defends Gritty Portrayal of Street Life, Admits 'Kingdom Come' and Retirements May Have Been Mistakes." Rock & Roll Daily, October 11, 2007. Retrieved November 27 (http://www.rollingstone.com/rockdaily).

Samuels, Allison. "The Reign of Jay-Z." *Newsweek*, November 22, 2004. Retrieved February 5, 2008 (http://www.newsweek.com/id/55779).

Sanneh, Kelefa. "A Show of Solidarity, with a Few Surprises." *New York Times*, October 29, 2005. Retrieved February 5, 2008 (http://www.nytimes.com/2005/10/29/arts/music/29jayz.html).

Scaggs, Austin. "Jay-Z: The Rolling Stone Interview." *Rolling Stone*, Issue 1040, November 29, 2007.

Strauss, Neil. "Rap Rules Among the Grammy Award Nominations." *New York Times*, December 5, 2003. Retrieved February 5, 2008 (http://www.nytimes.com).

INDEX

About the Author

Bridget Heos grew up in the 1980s, when *Yo MTV Raps!* was bringing hip-hop into middle-class Midwestern households like hers. She has always been interested in the criticism and defense of controversial language in rap music. For her, the most inspiring part of Jay-Z's story was that he never stopped writing and never gave up on his dream. He wrote honestly about his life. That takes courage!

Ms. Heos writes on a variety of nonfiction topics for teens and lives in Missouri.

Photo Credits

Cover, pp. 1, 7, 13, 15, 29, 33, 38 © Getty Images; pp. 9, 17, 27, 31 © WireImage/Getty Images; pp. 20, 24 © FilmMagic/Getty Images.

Designer: Thomas Forget; Editor: Bethany Bryan
Photo Researcher: Marty Levick